Printed in Hong Kong
Copyright 1991 • Ken Hanley
Book Design: Joyce Herbst • Typesetting: Charlie Clifford
Frank Amato Publications
P.O. Box 82112 • Portland, Oregon 97282
(503) 653-8108 • FAX: (503) 653-2766
ISBN: 1-878175-05-X

California
FLY TYING
& FISHING
Guide

Ken Hanley

Frank Amato Publications

DEDICATION

To my wife Lucinda. For being my biggest fan, and toughest critic, yet always encouraging me to reach for the stars.

ACKNOWLEDGMENTS

The past two years have been a wonderful learning time for me due to the creation of this book. During that time I met many storybook characters and a few top flight professionals. In each case the encouragement I received for this project gave me the motivation to take it yet another step forward. I didn't want the guide to be known as "one man's view," thus I sought the knowledge of other anglers to compile the most complete resource. Impromptu sessions on the water, casual meetings in fly shops, business lunches, hours on the phone and invitations to friend's homes were all vehicles for brainstorming and then qualifying information. Opinions flew with facts. The conversations were always animated and colorful...and always worthwhile!

I'd like to especially thank Mark Freedman for his skillful tying, his commitment to quality, and his friendship (Cranefly larva, Buddy!).

Dan Blanton is a never-ending source of wisdom. Thanks Dan for welcoming me into your home and offering your expertise. And thanks also to the following: Steve Karlin and Craig Payne—the Wizkid Tech Team, Ralph Cutter, Wong, Brune, Lemons, Rosenthal, the legions of contacts at the Monterey Bay Aquarium, Elkhorn Slough, Moss Landing Marine Library, and the list goes on and on!

To all those who contributed—my sincere thanks...and special thanks to Donna and Sunshine for their generous contribution!

Contents

About The Author

From panfish to roosterfish Ken's angling adventures have taken him to numerous locations around the world. As a native son of the Golden State, he still enjoys the richness and diversity of his home waters. His introduction to fly fishing took place in the mid-1960s, in the hallowed waters of Yosemite's valley.

Since 1973 Ken's career has focused on the outdoors. He holds a master's degree in environmental education and is a consultant to the State Department of Education. As owner of Adventures Beyond, Ken and his staff have had the pleasure of working with over 5,000 students in the wilderness. Both sport and interpretive skills courses are offered through his organization.

As an artist his work has been exhibited in public and private collections, as well as professional and popular publications.

Currently Ken resides in the San Francisco Bay area with his wife Lucinda and daughter Sierra.

Preface

Growing up in California has been a wondrous adventure. My life has been influenced a great deal by the state's natural beauty and diversity. The mountains and wilderness have become home to me, as well as the calling from the rugged coastline. I've chosen a lifestyle that allows me to share these magical places and their inhabitants with others. In concert with my teaching, artwork and writing are an integral part of this experience.

It's always a privilege to work with others on such a personal level. The quality time I've experienced with my students and clients has been profound. The natural environment has served as the rudimentary source for our collective wisdom. Our innate quality to impact on a single resource and the environment is extraordinary. California is unique, precious and vulnerable. Let's pull together...cheers to the future!

INTRODUCTION

Welcome to California fly fishing; with approximately 800 miles of surf zone and estuary waters for salt water angling, over two dozen streams and rivers holding salmon and steelhead, hundreds of lakes and streams in the High Sierra, hundreds of thousands of acres of bass waters, and a number of tailwater streams and spring creeks, California is a "first class" treasure house for fly fishing!

This pocket guide is intended as a reference tool for selecting appropriate fly patterns and sizes for the varied habitats and game fish of California. As with any "suggested" list, the reader is encouraged to delete or add patterns to fit their personal fly fishing style or specific waters.

Twelve habitats and their unique waters are represented. The following "eco-niches" include: Sierra Trout Streams, High Sierra Lakes (small surface area), Northern California Trout Streams, Surf-zone and Estuaries, North Coast Salmon/Steelhead Streams, Coastal Trout Stillwaters, Bass Stillwaters, Bay and Delta, Central Valley and Sierra Foothill Streams, Spring Creeks, California's Large Lakes, and Inshore Coastal Waters.

Each habitat has specific elements that require a fly fisher's attention. Weather, tide tables, and food chains are just a few examples of what must be considered when creating your fly selection.

Inshore Coastal Waters:

Variety! That's the one word that comes to mind when thinking about our inshore waters. Numerous game fish can be found in the diverse habitats off rock reefs, floating kelp beds, and sandy bottomed shallows. Food organisms are plentiful: predominantly squid, shrimp, crabs, anchovy and sardines. The "inshore" habitat exhibits a broad range. From surf line to five miles offshore, water depths vary from 10 feet to 100 feet or more. The intricate tides are a major factor in successful angling in this zone. The small craft fly fisher might do well to consider working the neap tides of each month. With such an expansive shoreline, California's Inshore Waters can be considered a powerhouse year-round fishery.

Dan Blanton

Primary Species:

Shark (blue, black tip), bass (kelp and sand), rockfish (black, blue, etc.), bonito, Pacific jack mackerel, kelp greenling, perch (kelp and pile), salmon.

Inshore Tidbits:

1. Rod selection: 8 through 11 weight, with enough backbone in the butt section to cast larger patterns and handle heavy fish.

2. Line selection: Shooting head system (Orvis Intermediate and Extra Fast Sinking), running line (Amnesia, Scientific Angler Intermediate, Cortland Plion, Orvis Braided), sink tip styles (Scientific Angler Wet-Tip IV/Hi-Speed Hi-D WF), floating styles (Cortland 444SL, L.L. Bean Bass Bug/Salt water Taper WF). Leaders are generally short and not tapered, instead they step down rather abruptly, a shock trace may be included.

3. Electronics are a distinct advantage in locating schools of fish, otherwise concentrate on "breaking zones"; edges of kelp beds, rock reefs, jetties, and pockets within floating kelp.

4. The fish here are visual feeders! Animation and color trigger feeding behavior. Lighter colored offerings work well at shallower depths. Consider using the Lime Punch for deeper water. Without much light penetration beyond 20 feet, green and blue imitations have the ability to hold their color longer.

5. In deeper water your fly selection should address the following bait fish body types and colors: sardine, smelt, herring, mackerel, anchovy, young boccaccio and other immature rockfish. Squid is always on the menu.

6. Sandy shallows and rocky habitat usually house large populations of crustaceans. Crab and shrimp flies should be considered high on the list.

7. Jack smelt are "plankton feeders" staying close to the surface...they are excellent game for dry fly fishing on calmer waters.

FLY PATTERNS

Sample waters: Santa Cruz and Monterey kelp beds, Channel Islands

Blanton's Sar-Mul-Mac, anchovy (streamer)	1/0 - 4/0	Year-round
Lefty's Deceiver, Blue (streamer)	1/0 - 4/0	Year-round
Blanton's King Harbor Bucktail (streamer)	2 - 1/0	Year-round
Blanton's Sar-Mul-Mac, mullet (streamer)	1/0 - 4/0	Year-round
Blanton's Sea Arrow Squid (streamer)	3/0	Year-round
Blanton's Tropical Punch (streamer)	1/0 - 3/0	Year-round
Lefty's Deceiver, White (streamer)	1/0 - 4/0	Year-round
Lefty's Deceiver, Yellow (streamer)	1/0 - 4/0	Year-round
Blanton's Lime Punch (streamer)	1/0 - 4/0	Year-round

Surf Zone And Estuaries:

The "surf zone" is a medley of environments, composed primarily of the surf line, tide pools, finger reefs and surf grass beds. The most thorough way to work in these areas is by wading and casting blind into a likely hot spot or sighting fish working the surface; the challenges are many and it takes a perceptive angler to cash in on the bounty. The game fish are "ocean-charged" and when the bite is on...it sizzles.

A rising spring tide is extremely productive. Estuaries are bodies of water that exist as bridges between the salt and fresh water worlds. Neap tides (with minimal rise and fall) usually produce a greater number of game fish in a short, concentrated time. Incoming tides tend to drive fish farther into the estuary or under cover.

Wading or casting from a small boat can put you into the action. The most significant food organisms, in either the surf zone or estuaries, are shrimp, crabs, and tiny bait fish.

Primary Species:
Surf perch (red tail, barred, silver, walleye, striped), rubberlip sea perch, spotfin croaker, kelp greenling, California cor-

bina, steelhead and salmon (see special section "North Coast Salmon and Steelhead Streams").

Surf Zone and Estuary Tidbits:
1. Rod selection: 7 through 9 weight, nine foot in length or better. Your rod should have enough character to handle the combined pressures of the hydraulic effect from the surf, plus the game fish and any extra debris. There is a lot of "salad in the soup" (floating kelp, surf grass, etc.).
2. Line selection: Sink tip styles (Cortland 444SL, Orvis Hy-Flote, Teeny Nymph), "mini" lead-heads, running line (Orvis Braided, Scientific Angler AirCel Floating or Intermediate). You might find unique opportunities in the tide pools for using a floating line. Leaders are generally short.
3. Often you will be casting into the wind which always increases from midday into the evening.
4. Perch are mostly bottom feeders—using a technique known as "oral winnowing," they take in small amounts of sand and debris and eject unwanted matter. There is no clear data on the feeding habits of perch within the surf line...remember, each wave stirs the sand and suspends food organisms so work your fly from bottom to top. From time to time you will see fish feeding in the surface foam between wave action.
5. When you explore tide pools look for ponds, channels, shelves, anything that might indicate a route of travel or a feeding station. Most game will stay close to cover.
6. Large populations of redtail perch, which can grow to 16 inches and a few pounds, are found throughout northern coastal waters. Variety in species is more likely to happen in the central and southern surf zones.

FLY PATTERNS

Sample waters: Dunes Beach, Elk Horn Slough, and Kings Harbor

Horner Shrimp (streamer)	4	Year-round
Polar Shrimp (wet)	6	Year-round
Krystal Bullet, Red (streamer)	4, 6	Year-round
Screamin' Shrimp, Fluorescent Orange (wet)	4, 6	Year-round
Surf Percher (wet)	4, 6	Year-round
Thor (wet)	6	Year-round
Blanton's Tropical Punch (streamer)	2/0	Year-round
Whitlock Purple Eelworm (streamer)	6	Year-round

Bay And Delta Regions:

The San Francisco Bay and its adjoining Delta system constitute the most extensive body of water throughout the state. Coupled with available food, the "built" or man made environment is the single largest factor for attracting and concentrating game fish. Bridges, docks and piers place high on the list. In addition, it's worth your time to explore backwater sloughs, shallow mud flats, and rocky shorelines which can all harbor healthy populations of fish. Larger fish feed heavily on smelt, herring, anchovy, and shrimp.

Using a boat is a distinct advantage in this environment. You can fish most of the habitat around-the-clock. Some of the best top-water action occurs during the night. Tides are again a concern. Generally, moving water is the key to success.

Dan Blanton

Primary Species:
Striped bass, black bass, pile perch, rubberlip perch, and jack smelt.

Bay and Delta Tidbits:
1. Rod selection: 9 through 11 weight. Heavier rods are used to pressure stripers near pilings and heavy structure.
2. Line selection: Shooting taper styles (Cortland 444SL No.4, Scientific Angler WetCel IV/Hi-Speed Hi-D), sink tip styles (Cortland 444SL, Orvis Hy-Flote or Easy Mend), running line (Amnesia, Scientific Angler Intermediate, Orvis Braided), floating styles (Scientific Angler AirCel ULTRA WF, 3M Mastery Saltwater Taper WF, Orvis SSS Hy-Flote, L.L. Bean Supra WF). Leaders are medium to short in length.
3. Striped bass are hungry for shad and shiner perch imitations. In early spring use smaller patterns—increase your hook size as the season progresses.
4. For stripers concentrate on waters from three to fifteen feet in depth. Pay particular attention to "built" shorelines (rip-rap of concrete and rock). Look for swirls, jumping bait fish or V-wakes to indicate bass feeding activity. Remember that stripers are constantly on the move.
5. Watch the birds! Cormorants, grebes and other expert divers can show you where the bait fish are. Predator species are usually not far behind.
6. The southwest Delta has excellent black bass opportunities during late fall and spring.

FLY PATTERNS

Sample waters: San Francisco Bay, Suison Bay, and San Joaquin Delta

Blanton's Bay Dredger (streamer)	2 - 3/0	Year-round
Blanton's Black Whistler Grizzly (streamer)	1/0 - 4/0	Year-round
Given's Barred N' White (streamer)	2 - 4/0	Year-round
Lefty's Deceiver, green (streamer)	1/0 - 4/0	Year-round
White Maribou Muddler (streamer)	2	Year-round
Blanton's Bay Delta Eelet (streamer)	1/0 - 4/0	Fall & Spring
Blanton's White Whistler (streamer)	1/0 - 4/0	Year-round
Blanton's White Whistler RG (streamer)	1/0 - 4/0	Year-round
Blanton's Yellow Whistler RG (streamer)	1/0 - 4/0	Year-round

North Coast Salmon And Steelhead Streams:

From small tidewater rivers to huge roaring waterways, the cold-water rivers and streams near the coast are spectacular. This is big fish country! Anadromous fish that is, born in fresh water but living over half their lives at sea. Weather plays a vital role in the design of this fishery.

Fall and winter rains swell the rivers and enable salmon and steelhead to gain access to their coveted spawning grounds. The colder water keeps these giants lively and on the move. High tides encourage the largest schools to enter fresh water.

The food organisms vary depending on where you are working in the river system. Closer to the mouth you might find shrimp and bait fish, while farther upstream salmon eggs, fry, caddis larva and stonefly nymphs dominate.

From flood stage to drought and anything in between, you must be prepared to travel when and where the fish do. Success means mobility.

Primary Species:
Steelhead trout, king (Chinook) salmon, silver (coho) salmon, and American shad.

Salmon and Steelhead Tidbits:

1. Rod selection: 6 through 9 weight.
2. Line selection: Sink tip styles (Orvis Hy-Flote or Easy Mend, Scientific Angler Wet Tip Steelhead, Teeny Shooting/Floating), floating styles (Orvis Salmon/Steelhead or SSS Hy-Flote, Scientific Angler AirCel ULTRA Weight Forward Steelhead, Cortland 444 Shooting Tapers). Carry a full range of leaders.
3. Small patterns are effective on coast waters. Down-size your fly and it might just give you the edge you need. Near tidewater steelhead and salmon still react to the salt water food chain—bait fish and crustacean imitations are appropriate. As you travel farther upstream, concentrate on "spawn style" egg patterns and fresh water food organisms such as nymph and larva imitations.
4. Winter-run salmon are "off the bite" in fresh water. They have no requirement to continue to feed as they move upstream. They are driven to spawn. Pacific salmon spawn one time and after they complete the act their life comes to an end. Kings are tough to coax into a strike, however silvers are a bit more willing to chase your streamer, especially when they are in an estuary environment.
5. Steelhead are multi-spawners and as a result are more apt to take your fly. Early season steelhead, in summer and fall, generally eat more when migrating than their winter-run cousins.

FLY PATTERNS

Sample waters: Klamath River, Eel River, and Garcia River:

Boss (wet)	4, 6, 10, 12	Sept.-March
Brindle Bug (wet)	6, 8, 10	Sept.-March
Burlap (wet)	6, 8, 10	Sept.-March
Double Egg Sperm (wet)	4	Dec.-Feb.
Fall Favorite (wet)	6	Sept.-March
Glo Bugs (egg)	6	Dec.-Feb.
Gold or Silver Comet (wet)	4, 6	Dec.-March
Krystal Bullet, Green (wet)	6, 8	Jan.-March
Silver Hilton (wet)	6, 8, 10	Sept.-March
Prince Nymph (nymph)	10, 12	Sept.-March
Martinez Black (nymph)	10, 12	Sept.-March

Coastal Stillwaters:

Our coastal stillwaters wear a variety of different hats: fresh water lagoons, metropolitan parks with lakes, and foothill lakes. You might consider their size as having that "personal" touch.

Surrounded by sand dunes and tules, lagoons are home to rainbows and steelhead; some waters house silver and king salmon as well. Fluctuating tides and rains trigger the fish's movement. Rainbow trout are sometimes present due to planting programs of the California Department of Fish and Game and others. Redwood stands and oak woodlands grace the countryside surrounding the foothill lakes. Sophisticated management programs, like the trophy trout fishery of Lake Lagunitas, make fly fishing a real joy in some of these waters. Metropolitan parks offer a combination of both warm and cold water species. They are readily accessible and often contain good populations of game fish. Food organisms such as bait fish, caddisflics and shrimp are sometimes abundant.

Primary Species:
Rainbow trout, steelhead trout, salmon, bass, and panfish.

Coastal Stillwater Tidbits:
1. Rod selection: 4 through 9 weight.
2. Line selection: Floating styles (L.L. Bean Bass Bug/Salt water Taper, Teeny Shooting/Floating, Cortland 444SL Bass Bug Taper, weight forward or double taper lines from Orvis and Scientific Angler), sink tip styles (L.L. Bean Wet Tip, Teeny Nymph, Scientific Angler AirCel Wet-Tip III/Hi-D). Carry a full range of leaders.
3. Work your nymphs...S-L-O-W-L-Y!
4. Panfish generally won't work that hard to feed. Don't over animate your fly, give it the lazy look. A slight twitch and long pause should get their interest.
5. Fish usually congregate around trees for a number of reasons—shade at midday, cover in the root system or sweeper branches, and the food produced around the tree's environment. A breeze blowing from shore to open water can carry insects blown off a tree. Position yourself to cast into and along the edges of the floating debris.
6. Many lakes offer boat rental programs. Expand your skills and learn the proper casting and fish handling techniques for working from small craft such as canoes and prams.
7. Large crappie are feeding on top during the pre-spawn (approximately mid-February to early March) and pre-summer (approximately late April to mid-May) time frames. Insect hatches and minnows are on the rise, water temperatures become compatible with shallows habitat, and aggressive behavior around nests are all a plus for fly rodders.

FLY PATTERNS

Sample waters: Lake Earl, Lake Lagunitas, and Lake Merced:

Damselfly (dry)	10	June-August
Marabou Damsel (nymph)	10, 12	May-August
Soft Hackles, "Limes" and "Pheasant Tail" (wet)	14, 16	May-Oct.
Henryville Special (dry)	14, 16	May-Oct.
Janssen Callibaetis (nymph)	14, 16	May-Oct.
Janssen Leech (wet)	8	April-Oct.
Scud (wet)	14	April-Oct.
Matthew's Sparkle Dun, Tan or Gray (dry)	16, 18	July-Oct.
Horner Shrimp (streamer)	4	Sept.-Feb.

Bass Stillwaters

What makes California bass waters so unique? North state waters are colder, their structure is usually natural, and angling hours are close to unlimited. A few of these northern lakes currently hold the record for trophy sized bass! Southern waters have a longer growing season (resulting in trophy sized fish), man-made structure is the rule, and impoundments account for a great many lakes. You can fish virtually any kind of water you choose, from private farm ponds to large lakes with 150 miles of shoreline or more.

Fly fishers do well during spring and fall seasons. Summer months are less kind to those casting fur and feathers, but still produce quality action during late evenings. Food organisms are a veritable smorgasbord and include threadfin shad, crawdads, waterdogs, small trout, insect larva and nymphs.

Primary Species:
Largemouth bass, spotted bass, smallmouth bass, white bass, crappie, and bluegill.

Bass Stillwater Tidbits:
1. Rod selection: 6 through 9 weight. Consider the fact that you might have to pull fish through heavy structure and cover.
2. Line selection: Floating styles (3M Mastery Bass Bug Taper WF, Cortland 444SL Bass Bug Taper, L.L. Bean Bass Bug Taper, Orvis Saltwater Taper, standard weight forward lines), sink tip styles (Teeny Nymph, Orvis Easy-Mend, Scientific Angler AirCel IV/Hi-Speed Hi-D), sinking styles (Scientific Angler WetCel II, Orvis Intermediate and Fast Sink). Leaders are typically short to medium length.
3. Consider the shape of the bass: large fins, short and thick body, huge mouth. They are supremely built to ambush prey in cover. Don't expect a bass to chase the offering very far. It's to your advantage to anticipate immediate action on any cast. Placement and accuracy produce "heavy" results!
4. The fly's size and silhouette is of primary importance. How you impart life to the imitation is critical. Color is the least of your worries, yet you still need to address the issue. Try this strategy for starters: black or deep opaque colors for darker water, yellow/green combinations in slightly off-color water, light, flashy colors for top water action and/or clear water.
5. During the night larger bass are cruisin' for a brusin'! Cooling surface water brings them up from deep cover. A full-moon night can be magic with a popper.

FLY PATTERNS

Sample waters: Lake Berryessa, Lake Casitas, and Pyramid Lake:

Mouse (dry)	4	April-Nov.
Dahlberg Diver (streamer)	6, 8	Jan.-Sept.
Janssen's Threadfin Shad (streamer)	6	June-Sept.
Whitlock Crayfish (wet)	8	Jan.-Sept.
Whitlock Black/Ann (popper)	6	Jan.-Sept.
Whitlock Purple Eelworm (streamer)	6	Jan.-Oct.
Zonker Natural (streamer)	6	June-Sept.
Hard Body Popper Frog Pattern	2	April-August

Central Valley And Sierra Foothill Streams:

Trout are on tap year-round. Winter months bring in anadromous species, with continuing runs through spring. Smallmouth explode from mid-spring into early fall. Casting a fly into these waters can provide action almost any time during the year.

Remember the scout's motto "be prepared." However, keep it in perspective. It's easy to overwhelm yourself with equipment and multiple locations. With so many species to angle for, it's best to single out your favorite on any given outing, and concentrate your tackle and techniques to obtain a higher percentage of hook-ups.

Long, extensive river systems characterize this region. Again the "mobility factor" applies to success. Drift boats, canoes, and motor boats increase the chance of fishing prime waters. Key food organisms include caddisflies, minnows, stoneflies, mayflies and of course eggs during spawning seasons.

Primary Species:
Rainbow trout, brown trout, smallmouth bass, American shad, striped bass, salmon and steelhead (see special section "North Coast Salmon and Steelhead Streams").

Central Valley and Sierra Foothill Tidbits:

1. Rod selection: 4 through 9 weight.
2. Line selection: Floating styles (Orvis WF, Scientific Angler AirCel ULTRA WF or DT, L.L. Bean Supra WF or DT), sink tip styles (Scientific Angler AirCel Wet-Tip IV/Hi-Speed Hi-D, Orvis Hy-Flote, Cortland 444SL). Carry a full range of leaders.
3. Shooting heads are generally the rule for shad. The across and down, swing technique, produces quite often at the bottom of the swing.
4. Smallmouth tend to favor rock walls and deadfall. Crawdad patterns are a favorite, as are Zonkers and stonefly nymphs.
5. Don't forget to explore the small dredger-ponds alongside many valley streams.
6. Spring run-off usually swells and colors foothill streams. With these conditions use your sink tip and pull larger streamers through back eddies and pools.
7. Look for hungry steelhead to start showing up during salmon spawning in the fall. *Small* Glo-Bug patterns, which imitate salmon eggs, are the most popular choice Variety in color is essential because the fish can be finicky eaters.
8. Because many rivers in this region are controlled by dams, water releases and river flows are an important aspect to successful angling. Keep in contact with local shops or guide services to find out recommended and current CFS (cubic feet per second) levels.

FLY PATTERNS

Sample waters: Stanislaus River, Feather River, and Merced River:

Adams (dry)	14, 16	April-Nov.
Goddard Caddis (dry)	14	July-Sept.
Griffith's Gnat (dry)	16 - 22	Year-round
Sculpin (streamer)	4	Year-round
LaFontaine's Emergent Sparkle Pupa (nymph)	14, 16	Year-round
Tan Elk Hair Caddis (dry)	14, 16	Year-round
Zonker Natural (streamer)	8, 10	April-Nov.
Shadfly: chartreuse, orange, red (streamer)	4, 6	May-June
Crawdad	2 - 8	April-Oct.
Black Stone (nymph)	4 - 6	April-July

High Sierra Trout Streams:

Sierra trout are a hearty bunch. Their home is a land of extremes. During winter months freezing temperatures and blankets of snow dominate the habitat. Spring finds rivers and streams swollen by a melting snowpack. Summer is a short season at best. Fall, again, brings the frost. Why fish the Sierras? Because it's a fly fisher's paradise. Beautiful colored fish, challenging waters, abundant wildlife, great scenery and solitude; it all adds up to quality time.

The boulder strewn character of the western slope creates a perfect breeding ground for caddis and stoneflies. The eastern waters, and their slower meandering character yield prolific mayfly hatches. Pocket-water, riffles, undercut banks...you name it and the Sierra has it.

Throughout the mountains the food organisms are classic: caddisflies, stoneflies, mayflies, terrestrials (ants, grasshoppers), midges and damselflies.

Primary Species:
Brook trout, rainbow trout, brown trout, and cutthroat trout.

High Sierra Trout Stream Tidbits:
1.   Rod selection: 3 through 7 weight.
2.   Line selection: Floating styles (Orvis WF, Scientific Angler AirCel ULTRA WF or DT, L.L. Bean Supra WF or DT), sinking styles (Scientific Angler WetCel Uniform Sink II or WetCel Intermediate, Orvis Intermediate), sink tip styles (Orvis WF, Cortland Floating Nymph-Tip). Carry a full range of leaders.
3.   There are a number of significant insects throughout the season from April to November; here are a few to get you started: Early season—Mayfly: blue winged olive, green drake, Callibaetis. Caddisfly: Green rock worm, spotted sedge, little tan sedge. Stonefly: Salmonfly, little yellow stone, golden. Miscellaneous: Midge. Mid-to late-season—Mayfly: Pale morning dun, blue winged olive, Trico. Caddisfly: Green rock worm, little tan sedge, little western dark, giant orange sedge. Stonefly: Little yellow stone, golden. Miscellaneous: Midges, ants, and hoppers.
4.   In most situations it's not necessary to make a long cast. These waters are intimate and tricky. If you have the ability to position yourself along the bank or wade to a good casting station this should keep you into fish.
5.   Slow streams altered by beaver activity offer some of the most exciting visual fishing in the mountains. Study the situation first because these fish can see your every move. It's a classic encounter and worth the extra attention.

FLY PATTERNS

Sample waters: Truckee River, Carson River, and Yosemite Creek

Adams (dry)	14, 16	June-Nov.
Fur Ants (black and cinnamon)	10 - 16	August-Nov.
Cutter's Perfect Ant	10 - 16	June-Sept.
Bird's Nest (nymph)	10, 12, 14	June-Sept.
Crowe Beetle	14, 16	July-Sept.
Gold Ribbed Hare's Ear (nymph)	8 - 16	June-Oct.
Dave's Hopper	6, 8	August-Oct.
Green Caddis Larva (nymph)	12, 14	April-Oct.
Little Yellow Stone (dry)	14, 16	June-Aug.
Cutter's Tangerine Dream (nymph)	6, 8	Sept. & Oct.
Parachute Hare's Ear (dry)	14, 16	June-Nov.
Polly's Casual Dress (nymph)	8 - 14	June-Nov.
Royal Wulff (dry)	12, 14	June-Sept.
LaFontaine's Emergent Sparkle Pupa	12, 14	April-Nov.
Tan Elk Hair Caddis (dry)	12, 14	June-Oct.
Woolly Bugger (streamer)	6 - 10	June-Nov.
Yellow Humpy (dry)	12, 14	June-Oct.

High Sierra Lakes (Small Surface):

S ierra stillwaters are a harsh environment by anyone's standard. Yet they house incredible jewels like the golden trout. In many cases—gouged out by ancient glaciers—the smaller waters are crystal clear, ice cold, and relatively free from heavy bottom vegetation. Rock islands and deadfall logs assume much of the structure you'll come across. Debris brought in by feeder streams can change the personality of a lake in a single season.

From high water mark to a mere puddle, the season's grip on the watershed is a potent factor in the composition of alpine stillwater. The bite during ice-out can be red hot. An evening hatch during mid-summer can turn the surface into a popcorn popper. The sun's warming rays in the early morning bring fish into the shallows to sip in the film.

The diminutive midge is a heavyweight in this realm. Caddisflies, mayflies and damselflies join in, as do scuds, snails, terrestrials and minnows.

Primary Species:
Brook trout, rainbow trout, golden trout, and cutthroat trout.

Sierra Lakes Tidbits:
1. Rod selection: 5 through 7 weight.
2. Line selection: Floating styles (Orvis WF, Scientific Angler AirCel ULTRA WF or DT, L.L. Bean Supra WF or DT), sinking styles (Scientific Angler WetCel Uniform Sink II or III, L.L. Bean Supra I) sink tip styles (Orvis WF, Cortland Floating Nymph-Tip or 444SL). Carry a full range of leaders.
3. Stillwater hatches vary from stream born insects quite often. There are a few insects found in both moving and stillwater environs, yet their emergence cycles might vary. Early season—Mayfly: Callibaetis, pale morning dun. Caddisfly: Spotted sedge. Miscellaneous: Alderfly and midge. Mid- to late-season—Mayfly: Callibaetis, blue winged olive, Trico, pale morning dun. Caddisfly: American grannom, spotted sedge. Miscellaneous: Midge and damselfly.
4. First concentrate your efforts on cruising lanes instead of holding lies. Ledges, weedbed and flotsam lines, along deadfalls, around rocky points—any of these can be prime zones for feeding fish. Work deeper waters and holding lies as the sun and water temperatures rise.
5. Pay attention to wind seams on the surface. Wind tends to create concentrations of rafting food organisms (as during a spinner fall); fish will position themselves to take advantage of the easy pickings.

FLY PATTERNS

Sample waters: Martis Lake, Lake of the Woods, and Meiss Lake:

Black Midge (dry)	20, 22	April-Nov.
Marabou Damsel (nymph)	10	June-July
Damsel Fly (dry)	10,12	June-July
Henryville Special (dry)	16	July-Sept.
Janssen Callibaetis (nymph)	14, 16	June-Sept.
Kaufmann's Chironomid (pupa and larva)	18, 20	April-Nov.
Light Cahill (dry)	16	July-Oct.
Cutter's Martis Midge (emerger)	14	June-Sept.
Light Tan Spinner (dry)	14 - 18	July-Sept.
Callibaetis (Speckled Dun) Pheasant Tail (nymph)	16	June-Oct.
Tan Elk Hair Caddis (dry)	14	July-Sept.
Scud (wet)	14, 16	July-Sept.
Matthew's Sparkle Dun (dry) or		
Callibaetis (Speckled Dun)	16, 18	July-Oct.
Woolly Bugger (streamer)	8	June-Oct.
Blanton's Flash Tail series (streamer)	2 - 8	April-Nov.
Dark and Light Kaufmann's Timberline (emerger)	12, 16	June-Sept.
Olive or brown		

Spring Creeks:

The waters are cool and loaded with oxygen. The banks typically undercut. The flow is constant and gentle. The creek bottoms covered in thick carpets of weed. There's food from top to bottom...everywhere!

Known for their legendary mayfly hatches, spring creeks have become the dry fly fisher's habitat of choice. Dreams of a 20 inch trout raising through the film to a size 20 Trico can be a reality. As for nymph fishing, those luxurious weedbeds play host to a number of tasty morsels sought after by hungry trout. The intricate bank structure and subtle subsurface currents present their own unique set of challenges. Small watercraft and bank angling are successful approaches. Wading can be difficult and requires a thoughtful presence to minimize environmental impact.

The predominant food organisms are mayflies, scuds, leeches, minnows, terrestrials, caddisflies and stoneflies.

Primary Species:
Rainbow trout and brown trout.

Spring Creek Tidbits:
    1. Rod selection: 2 through 6 weight. Use lighter rods for super selective trout and tiny flies. The 5 or 6 weight models allow you to handle heavier nymphs, wind, and long roll casts.
    2. Line selection: Floating styles (Scientific Angler AirCel ULTRA WF or DT, Cortland 444SL DT, Orvis WF), sink tip styles (Orvis WF, Scientific Angler AirCel Wet-Tip II or III). Carry a full range of leaders.
    3. Downstream or down and across presentations are highly effective.
    4. Line indicators will help you detect subtle nymph feeding trout.
    5. In a pinch parachute style patterns can be used to imitate mayfly spinners.
    6. Significant hatches include: Early Season: Mayfly— Pale morning dun, green drake, blue winged olive, and Trico. Stonefly: Salmonfly. Caddisfly: Spotted and olive sedge. Mid- to late-season: Mayfly—Trico, Hexagenia, and blue winged olive. Caddisfly: Giant orange sedge. Stonefly: Little yellow stone.
    7. After a hatch occurs try your hand at working the undercuts along the banks. Search out holding lies where big fish settle in.

FLY PATTERNS

Sample Waters: Fall River, Hot Creek, and Hat Creek

Fur Ant, black	10, 14, 18	June-Oct.
Blue Winged Olive (dry)	16, 18	April/May-Sept./Nov.
Parachute style or Matthew's Sparkle Dun or		
Dave's Hopper	6, 8	August-Sept.
Green Drake Paradrake (dry)	10	June, July, Oct.
Griffith's Gnat (dry)	14 - 20	April-Nov.
Hexagenia Paradun (dry)	6	June-July
Janssen Leech (streamer)	6, 8	April-Nov.
Pheasant Tail (nymph)	16 - 20	May-Oct.
Spinners, Poly-winged (dry)	16 - 22	May-Oct.
May substitute with "Hen" winged or "Antron"		
Quiggly Cripple (dry)	16 - 20	May-Oct.
Scud (nymph)	14	June-Sept.
Trico (dry)	18 - 24	August-Oct.
Zug Bug (nymph)	14 - 18	May-Nov.
Pale Morning Dun (dry)	16 - 20	June-Nov.
Parachute style or Matthew's Sparkle Dun		

NORTHERN TROUT STREAMS:

The fish are strong, thick bodied and beautiful fighters. The trout of this region enjoy an international reputation. The genetics of the McCloud River strain account for many of the rainbows found in international waters. An added benefit of these river systems are the migrations of trout from nearby lakes. Large browns and rainbows enter the rivers to spawn, providing a boost to native populations.

The northern streams are classic freestone habitats. Boulders and small rocks constitute most of the streambed. Riffles, pools, and pocketwater provide great angling. Wading is the ticket for success. Caddisflies and stoneflies provide much of the action, as do minnows, mayflies and terrestrials.

Primary Species:
Rainbow trout and brown trout.

Northern Stream Tidbits:

1. Rod selection: 5 through 7 weight.
2. Line selection: Floating styles (Scientific Angler AirCel ULTRA WF or DT, Cortland 444SL DT, Orvis WF), sink tip styles (Orvis WF, Scientific Angler AirCel Wet-Tip III). Carry a full range of leaders.
3. Short line nymphing is a popular method on these waters.
4. October and November bring in huge spawning browns.
5. Your fly box should be pro caddis and stonefly imitations. Summer months offer the best evening hatches.
6. Hatches to look for: Stonefly: Salmonfly, little yellow stone, golden stone. Caddisfly: Spotted, American grannom, little tan short-horned, giant orange sedge. Mayfly: Pale morning dun, Callibaetis, blue winged olive.
7. Faster waters usually hold smaller trout, and sometimes they are there in quantity. Look for larger fish to hold in pocketwater and near the banks.
8. Heavy early season rains can blowout a river overnight. Be prepared for cool, wet weather anytime. Strong currents demand your attention; carry a wading staff and use the buddy system.

FLY PATTERNS

Sample Waters: Upper Sacramento and McCloud rivers.

Adams (dry)	12, 14, 16	May-Nov.
Elk Hair Caddis, tan (dry)	14	May-Oct.
Golden Stone (nymph)	8	May-July
Light Cahill (dry)	14, 16	May-Oct.
Little Yellow Stone (dry)	14	May-Sept.
Muddler Minnow (streamer)	6, 8, 10	April-Nov.
Kaufmann's Stimulator (dry)	6	Oct.
Cutter's Tangerine Dream (nymph)	6, 8	Sept.-Oct.
Pheasant Tail (nymph)	14, 16	May-Oct.
Prince Nymph (nymph)	10	April-Nov.
Sculpin (streamer)	4	June-Oct.
Woolly Worm (nymph)	6, 8	May-Nov.
Yellow Humpy (dry)	14	June-Sept.
Black Stone (nymph)	4, 6	April-June
Yellow Jacket (dry and wet)	10, 12	June-Sept.

CALIFORNIA'S LARGE LAKES:

What can we say about these lakes? How about colossal, copious, enormous, and grand for starters. Would you believe surface areas from 11,000 to 43,000 acres plus in good water years? How do you approach such an expanse with a fly rod? Try fishing it like a small lake. Reduce the surface acres into mini-waters. Flats, sloughs, deep blue water, islands, shoreline structure—there's a wealth of habitat to explore. Boats clearly allow the angler an advantage in covering these areas. How about carrying a float tube onboard, and using it to fine-tune specific locations?

Food organisms include crawdads, scuds, leeches, and insect hatches (to a lesser degree). Minnows bring on the real predator/prey relationships in large lakes—tiny fish eaten by bigger fish, eaten by larger fish, eaten by even larger fish.

Primary Species:

Rainbow trout, brown trout, largemouth bass, spotted bass, smallmouth bass, kokanee salmon, and lake trout.

Large Lake Tidbits:

1. Rod selection: 7 through 9 weight.

2. Line selection: Sink tip styles (Teeny Nymph, Orvis Hy-Flote, Cortland 444SL, Scientific Angler Wet-Tip IV/Hi-Speed Hi-D), shooting head styles (Cortland 444 No. 4, Orvis 38', Scientific Angler WetCel IV ST), running line (Orvis Braided, Amnesia), floating styles (Scientific Angler AirCel ULTRA WF, Orvis WF, L.L. Bean Supra WF). Carry a full range of leaders.

3. As the sun sets fish become more active at seeking food in the shallows and just under the surface.

4. Trolling streamers in a float tube can be an effective way to locate cruising fish. Use a stout leader because the strike from a big fish can be a real jolt.

5. When working a sub-surface fly (nymph or streamer), place your rod tip on or under the water's surface. This technique reduces slack in the system, dampens tip vibrations, and increases your sensitivity to the strike.

6. By using a thermometer attached to a drop line you can sometimes determine which species are on the bite and at what depth. Textbook temperatures read as follows: mid 50s—brookies, rainbows and salmon; 58 to 60—browns; low 70s—smallmouth and crappie; mid 70s—bluegill and largemouth bass.

FLY PATTERNS

Sample Waters: Lake Tahoe, Lake Almanor, and Clear Lake

Janssen Leech (streamer)	6	Year-round
Olive Matuka (streamer)	6, 8	Year-round
Scuds (wet)	12, 14	April-Sept.
Janssen's Threadfin Shad (streamer)	6	March-Nov.
Whitlock Crayfish (wet)	8	May-Sept.
Woolly Bugger (streamer)	6	Year-round
Zonkers (streamer)	6, 8	March-Nov.
Natural Blanton's Flash Tail Series (streamer) **Dark and Light**	2 - 8	Year-round

FLY PATTERNS

Flies tied by Mark Freedman
Photographed by
Jim Schollmeyer

ADAMS (Leonard Halladay)
Hook: *Size 14 - 16*
Thread: *Gray or black*
Wings: *Grizzly hackle tips*
Tail: *Grizzly and brown hackle fibers mixed*
Body: *Dubbed muskrat*
Hackle: *Brown and grizzly mixed*

BIRD'S NEST (Cal Bird)
Hook: *Size 10 - 16*
Thread: *Tan or brown*
Tail: *Mallard flank fibers, dyed bronze, sparse*
Ribbing: *Medium copper wire*
Body: *Fifty percent olive Australian opossum and 50 percent tan hare's ear*
Wing: *Mallard, dyed bronze, tied back to cover the body*
Thorax: *Same as body, tied full*

BLACK MIDGE
Hook: *Size 20 - 22*
Thread: *Black*
Tail: *Black hackle fibers*
Body: *Dubbed fur, black*
Hackle: *Black*

BLACK STONE NYMPH
(Randall Kaufmann)
Kaufmann Stone
Hook: *Tiemco 300, size 4 - 8*
Thread: *Black*
Tail: *Black goose biot*
Antennae: *Same as tail*
Ribbing: *Black Swannundaze*
Body: *Blended dubbing, black, dark brown*
Wingcase: *Three separate sections of lacquered turkey clipped to shape, each wingcase is tied in separately alternated with thorax fur*
Thorax: *Same as body*
Head: *Same as body*

BLANTON'S BAY DREDGER (Dan Blanton)

Hook: *Mustad 34007 (stainless) or 3407 (cadmium), size 2 - 3/0*
Thread: *White, size A Nymo or equivalent*
Optics: *Medium, silver bead chain, tie one-quarter inch from ring eye*
Underbody: *Wrap shank with No. 3 lead wire*
Body: *Gold mylar, wound flat*
Underwing: *Medium bunch of white bucktail, approximately 2 to 3 inches in length*
Overwing: *Green or blue bucktail, 15 to 25 strands, length of underwing*

Topping: *Six to eight strands of peacock herl, length of wing*
Head: *Should be half the hook shank in length. Build up with thread to full profile, add medium silver bead chain eyes just behind hook eye*

Attention:
1. Paint two red lines on underside of head, representative of gills

BLANTON'S SAR-MUL-MAC (Dan Blanton)

Mullet Version

Hook: *Mustad 3407 (cadmium) or 34007 (stainless), size 1/0 - 4/0*

Thread: *White, size A Nymo or equivilent*

Tail: *White bucktail, medium bunch, length optional*

Hackle Wing: *Six to nine white or yellow saddle hackles, tie in at halfway point on shank, do not tie in flared*

Wing Flash: *Six to eight silver or Flashabou mylar strips, half length of wing*

Underwing: *To form a belly, tie in medium bunch of white bucktail, length to bend of hook*

Overwing: *Two long grizzly saddle hackles, natural color or blue, green or yellow, as long or longer than wing hackles*

Collar: *Medium, Red chenille, two turns*

Head Topping: *Loop of gray chenille or 12 strands of peacock herl*

Optics: *4 to 8mm glass eyes, amber*

Head: *White or yellow medium chenille*

Attention:

1. To tie the "Anchovy Version," use blue or green bucktail and peacock hcrl for the overwing and topping

Dark Version
Hook: *Size 2 - 8*
Thread: *Green*
Tail: *Gold Flashabou*
Body: *Gold diamond braid or mylar tubing wrapped*

Hackle: *Dark green and grizzly dyed orange*
Wing: *"Peacock" green Krystal Flash*
Topping: *Peacock herl*

BLANTON'S FLASH TAIL SERIES (Dan Blanton)

White Version
Hook: *Size 2 - 8*
Thread: *White*
Tail: *Silver Flashabou*
Body: *Pearl Diamond Braid*
Hackle: *White*
Wing: *Dark green bucktail, sparse*

Topping: *Peacock herl*

Attention:
1. In both patterns, the wing should not extend any farther than half the length of the tail

Lime Punch
Hook: *Eagle Claw 254 CAT, size 2/0 - 3/0*
Thread: *Hot green, size A*
Optics: *Large silver bead chain eyes*
Tail: *Medium bunch of hot green bucktail*
Tail-Flash: *Twenty-five to 30 strands of green Flashabou per side*
Body: *Green mylar piping or green Krystal Hair, one turn under tail then wrap forward to within one-quarter inch of eyes*

Hackle: *Hot green saddle hackle, long and webby, five turns*
Topping: *Three parts, light green Krystal Hair, peacock Krystal Hair, peacock herl, 10-15 strands of each, stacked*
Wing: *Hot green grizzly saddle hackle to length of tail, one per side*
Head: *Medium, hot green chenille wrapped around bead chain eyes, topped with overlay of peacock herl*

BLANTON'S PUNCH SERIES (Dan Blanton)

Tropical Punch
Hook: *Eagle Claw 254 CAT, size 2/0 - 3/0*
Thread: *Hot orange, size A*
Optics: *Large silver bead chain eyes*
Tail: *Medium bunch of yellow bucktail*
Tail-Flash: *Twenty-five to 30 strands of gold Flashabou per side*
Body: *Gold mylar piping, one turn under tail then wrap forward to within one-quarter inch of eyes*

Hackle: *Yellow saddle hackle, long and webby, five or six turns*
Topping: *Three parts, yellow Krystal Hair, peacock Krystal Hair, peacock herl, 10-15 strands of each, stacked*
Wing: *Hot orange grizzly saddle hackle to length of tail, one per side*
Head: *Medium, hot orange chenille wrapped around eyes, topped with overlay of peacock herl*

White Whistler
Hook: *Mustad 9175, size 1/0 - 4/0*
Thread: *Red, size A Nymo or equivalent*
Optics: *Medium/large silver bead chain, weight hook with several turns of lead wire around shank behind the eyes, secure wire with thread*
Wing: *White bucktail, tie on in three bunches starting at rear of shank, clip butts to taper each bunch, stack for high vertical profile*
Median Line: *Thin line of red bucktail hairs to each side centered on the wing*
Body: *Two close turns of medium red chenille*
Hackle: *Three long webby white saddle hackles, spiral wrap, work one at a time to fill-in gap between body and eyes*

BLANTON'S WHISTLER SERIES (Dan Blanton)

Black Whistler Grizzly
Hook: *Mustad 9175, size 1/0 - 4/0*
Thread: *Black, size A Nymo or equivalent*
Optics: *Medium/large silver bead chain, weight hook around shank behind eyes, secure wire with thread*
Wing: *Black bucktail, three bunches. Add two grizzly hackle per side, one up and one down, splayed (refer to white R/G)*
Collar: *Medium, black chenille, two turns*
Hackle: *Three large, webby, black saddle hackles*

White Whistler R/G
Hook: *Mustad 9175, size 1/0 -4/0*
Thread: *Red, size A Nymo or equivalent*
Optics: *Medium/large silver bead chain, weight hook around shank behind eyes, secure wire with thread*
Wing: *White bucktail, three bunches. To each side add two natural grizzly hackles, flaring outward, one tilts upward the other tilts downward, same length as the bucktail. Hackles should follow the profile edges of the tail*
Body: *Two turns of medium red chenille*
Hackle: *Three of the widest marabou-style red hackles, spiral wrapped to fill gap between body and eyes, tie off*

Yellow Whistler R/G
Hook: *Mustad 9175, size 1/0 - 4/0*
Thread: *Red, size A Nymo or equivalent*
Optics: *Medium/large silver bead chain, weight hook around shank behind eyes, secure wire with thread*
Wing: *Yellow bucktail, two natural grizzly hackles per side, one up and one down, splayed (refer to white R/G)*
Body: *Red chenille*
Hackle: *Three of the widest marabou-style red hackles*

BLANTON'S KING HARBOR BUCKTAIL (Dan Blanton)

Hook: *Mustad 3407, size 2 - 1/0*
Thread: *Red*
Eyes: *Medium bead chain*
Tail: *White bucktail, sparse with 8 - 10 strands of silver Flashabou on each side*
Body: *Pearl Diamond Braid*
Hackle: *Large white saddle, folded*
Wing: *Four layers*
1st, White bucktail
2nd, Pearl Krystal Flash
3rd, Blue Krystal Flash
4th, Peacock herl

BLANTON'S BAY DELTA EELET (Dan Blanton)

Hook: *Mustad 3407 size 4/0*
Thread: *Black*
Eyes: *Medium silver bead chain, one quarter inch behind the hook eye*
Tail: *Medium sized bunch of black horse mane or artificial hair approximately 5 inches long. On both sides tie in 3 black saddle hackles of same length, do not splay*

Body: *Medium black chenille, wound to halfway point of body*
Wing: *Tie in 3 black narrow saddle hackles on each side. In addition, cover each side with a natural grizzly hackle*
Head: *Continue chenille forward, crisscross over the eyes, wind forward and tie down at the head*

40

BLANTON'S SEA ARROW SQUID (Dan Blanton)

Hook: *Eagle Claw 66-SS, size 2/0 - 4/0, straighten bend*
Thread: *White Nymo*
Tip: *Gold mylar, from halfway of bend to end of hook shank*
Butt: *Large white chenille wrapped to a ball*
Tail: *Eight white saddle hackles about 3 inches long as a wing, splayed, centered on each side, add one white saddle hackle about 5 inches long, centered add a few strands of coarse purple bucktail and purple Krystal Flash about 3 inches long*

Optics: *8mm glass eyes, amber, bend the wire to 90 degrees at each eye, tie in one at a time close to the shank*
Topping and Throat: *Fill the gap between the eyes with white marabou*

Body: *Build the body with cotton or floss, taper from eye to head, cover with medium/large white chenille, leave eighth-inch between body and hook eye*
Posterior Fin: *Two tufts of calf tail*

BLUE WINGED OLIVE
Parachute Version
Hook: *Size 16 - 18*
Thread: *Olive*
Wing: *Light elk hair*
Tail: *Dun hackle fibers*
Dubbing: *Light olive or olive gray dubbing*
Hackle: *Dun*

BOSS (Grant King)
Hook: *Size 4 - 12, weight to suit*
Thread: *Orange*
Tail: *Black bucktail, twice the length of body*
Ribbing: *Oval silver tinsel*
Body: *Black chenille*
Hackle: *Fluorescent orange, tied as a collar*
Eyes: *Silver bead chain*

BRINDLE BUG
Hook: *Size 6 - 10*
Thread: *Brown*
Tails: *One brown hackle tip*
Ribbing: *Oval silver tinsel*
Body: *Black and yellow variegated chenille*
Hackle: *Brown*

BURLAP
Hook: *Size 6 - 10, weight to suit*
Thread: *Tan*
Tail: *Coastal blacktail deer, body hair*
Body: *Burlap*
Hackle: *Grizzly*

CRANE FLY LARVA (Craig Matthews)
Hook: *Size 6 - 10, 4X long, weight to suit*
Thread: *Gray*
Tail: *Brown partridge*
Rib: *Clear "V" rib*
Body: *Olive/gray dubbing, thick*
Thorax: *Hare's mask dubbing*

CROWE BEETLE
Hook: *Size 14 - 18*
Thread: *Black*
Shell: *Black deer hair, pull forward over shank*
Body: *Black thread*
Legs: *Black deer hair fibers, three per side*
Head: *Clipped ends of excess deer hair*

CUTTER'S PERFECT ANT (Ralph Cutter)
Hook: *Size 10 - 16*
Thread: *Black*
Shellback: *Black deer*
Body: *Black or brown dubbing*
Wing: *Butt ends of shellback*
Hackle: *Ginger, tied parachute*
Head: *Black or brown dubbing*

Attention:
1. Tie in deer hair
2. Dub back half of hook only
3. Pull hair over to form shellback, post butt ends up
4. Wrap hackle parachute style
5. Trim butts close to hackle, use drop of head cement
6. Dub the head

CUTTER'S MARTIS MIDGE
(Ralph Cutter)
Hook: *Size 14*
Thread: *Olive*
Tail: *Pale Orange Krystal Flash, 4 strands, short*
Body: *Rusty orange dubbing, thin*
Wing: *Orange elk hair, do not flair*
Hackle: *Brown, 3 turns*

Attention:
1. Wing is posted at 45 degrees with tips extending forward, trim off butts leaving approximately one sixteenth inch extending over the body
2. Wrap the hackle inside the "V" formed by the wing and wing butts

CUTTER'S TANGERINE
DREAM (Ralph Cutter)
Hook: *Tiemco 200, size 8*
Thread: *Brown*
Body: *Rusty orange dubbing, "thick"*
Hackle: *Partridge or grouse, approximately three turns*

DAHLBERG DIVER,
Chartreuse (Larry Dahlberg)
Hook: *Size 6 - 8*
Thread: *Green*
Weedguard: *Hard nylon to match diameter of hook*
Body: *Silver Diamond Braid*
Wing: *Chartreuse rabbit strip*
Hackle and Collar: *Chartreuse deer hair*
Head: *Chartreuse deer hair, spun and clipped to shape*

DAMSEL FLY, DRY (Gary Borger)

Hook: *Size 10*
Thread: *Black*
Wing Post: *Blue deer hair*
Head and Body: *Blue deer hair, extended*

Ribbing: *Black tying thread*
Hackle: *Grizzly type, parachute, clipped in front*

DAVE'S HOPPER (Dave Whitlock)

Hook: *Size 6 - 8, 2X long*
Thread: *Gray*
Tail: *Dyed red deer hair, gap width in length*
Rib: *Brown hackle palmered*
Body: *Yellow yarn, small loop of yarn*
Underwing: *Yellow elk hair, to bend of hook*

Overwing: *Lacquered turkey wing quill section, trimmed to shape, or ringneck pheasant "church window" feather, lacquered to shape*
Hackle and Head: *Natural deer hair, spun and clipped to shape*

DOUBLE EGG SPERM

Hook: *Size 4*
Thread: *Fluorescent fire orange*
Tail: *Golden pheasant crest or yellow hackle fibers*
Body: *Hot pink chenille, two balls,* *band of gold embossed tinsel separates the body at center of hook*
Hackle: *Hot pink*
Wing: *White marabou*

ELK HAIR CADDIS, Tan (Al Troth)

Hook: *Size 14 - 16*
Thread: *Tan*
Ribbing: *Gold wire*
Body: *Tan or brown dubbing*
Hackle: *Brown*
Wing: *Tan cream elk hair*

FALL FAVORITE (Butch Wilson)

Hook: *Size 6*
Thread: *Red*
  Body: *Embossed silver tinsel*

Hackle: *Scarlet red*
Wing: *Hot orange calf tail*

FUR ANT

Black Fur Ant
Hook: *Size 10 - 16*
Thread: *Black*
Body: *Dubbed black fur, two small balls, rear portion slightly larger*

Hackle: *Black, sparse, tied in at center joint of body*

Cinnamon Fur Ant
Tied same as black except materials are cinnamon brown

GIVEN'S BARRED N' WHITE (Ed Givens)

Hook: *Mustad 34007 or 3407 Cadmium, size 2 - 4/0*
Thread: *White, Nymo size A*
Optics: *Medium silver bead chain eyes, one-eight to one-quarter inch behind hook eye*
Body: *Wrap 3 inch lead wire, cover with tying thread*
Tail: *White saddle hackle, long and webby, three per side, splayed*

Wing: *White bucktail, medium size bunches tied top bottom and sides, extending past hook bend*
Topping and Throat: *Large grizzly neck hackles, one per side top and bottom, splayed, half the length of the tail*
Hackle: *Red saddle hackle, full*
Head: *Tying thread, large and tapered*

GLO BUG

Hook: *Mustad 9174 or 9479, size 2 - 6*
Thread: *Kevlar thread of appropriate color*

Body: *Glo Bug yarn, flared and trimmed to salmon egg shape.*

48

**GODDARD CADDIS
(John Goddard and
Andre Puyans)**
Hook: *Size 14*
Thread: *Brown*
Body: *Natural deer hair, spun and trim-
med*
Antennae: *Stripped hackle stem from
brown hackle feather*
Hackle: *Brown*

GOLD RIBBED HARE'S EAR
Hook: *Tiemco 200, size 8 - 16, weighted*
Thread: *To match body*
Tail: *Hare's mask fibers*
Ribbing: *Gold wire or oval tinsel*
Body: *Dubbed hare's mask, shaggy*
Wingcase: *Dark turkey tail*
Thorax: *Same as body*

GOLD COMET
Hook: *Size 4 - 6*
Thread: *Orange*
Tail: *Orange bucktail or calf tail*
Body: *Gold Diamond Braid*
Hackle: *Yellow and orange mixed*
Eyes: *Brass bead chain*

GOLDEN STONE (Randall Kaufmann)

Hook: *Tiemco 300, size 2 - 10, weighted and flattened*
Thread: *Yellow*
Tail: *Strip goose dyed yellow*
Antennae: *Strip goose dyed yellow*
Rib: *Yellow Swannundaze*
Body: *Mixture of (50 percent) angora goat and (50 percent) Hairtron, golden-brown*

Wingcase: *Lacquered turkey, three separate sections, alternated with thorax fur, wingcase should be one-half length of hook shank*
Thorax: *Same as body*
Head: *Same as body*

GREEN CADDIS LARVA

Hook: *Size 10 - 16*
Thread: *Black*
Body: *Fluorescent green dubbing, twisted*

Legs: *Brown partridge or grouse*
Head: *Brown or black dubbing*

GREEN DRAKE PARADRAKE (Mike Lawson)

Hook: *Size 10 or 12*
Thread: *Yellow*
Wing: *Dark blue dun*
Tail: *Moose body hair*

Body: *Olive elk*
Ribbing: *Yellow tying thread*
Hackle: *Grizzly dyed yellow or olive*

GRIFFITH'S GNAT

Hook: *Size 14 - 20*
Thread: *Black*

Body: *Peacock herl*
Hackle: *Grizzly, palmered*

HARD BODY POPPER Frog Pattern Version

Hook: *37187 Mustad, Stinger, size 6*
Thread: *Black*
Legs: *Grizzly dyed olive*
Hackle: *Black, large and webby, tied off
at halfway point on shank*

Body: *Balsawood, formed to shape,
painted green with yellow dots,
shape front end as cupped mouth
and paint red*

◆◆◆◆◆◆

HENRYVILLE SPECIAL

Hook: *Size 16*
Thread: *Brown*
Ribbing: *Grizzly tied palmered over
body*
Body: *Olive wool yarn or dubbing*
Underwing: *Barred lemon wood duck
fibers, extend just past bend*

Wings: *Natural dark gray duck quill,
tied tent style, extending just past
the underwing*
Hackle: *Brown, sparse, 3 turns*

HEXAGENIA PARADUN

Hook: *Size 4 - 6*
Thread: *Yellow*
Wing: *Bleached Elk Hair*
Tail: *Bleached Elk Hair*

Body: *Pale Yellow or Bleached Elk*
Ribbing: *Yellow tying thread*
Hackle: *Ginger, parachute*

HORNER SHRIMP   (Jack Horner)

Hook: *Size 4, weight to suit*
Thread: *Black*
Tail: *Natural bucktail*
Shellback: *Natural bucktail*
Body: *Oval silver tinsel, spiral wraps*

Hackle: *Grizzly tied palmered over the body, wrap the hackle before back is pulled over*
Eyes: *Painted white with black centers*

JANSSEN CALLIBAETIS NYMPH (Hal Janssen)

First Version
Hook: *Size 14 - 16, 2X Long*
Thread: *Olive*
Tail: *Golden pheasant tippet dyed olive*
Body: *Olive thread*

Over Body: *Strip of plastic (Zip-Loc Baggie)*
Wing Case: *Dark turkey*
Thorax: *Same as body*
Legs: *Woodduck*

Second Version
Hook: *Size 14 - 16, 2X Long*
Thread: *Olive*
Tail: *Golden Pheasant Tippet dyed olive, or suitable substitute*

Body: *Olive Brown dubbing (example: Sealex No. 109)*
Wing Case: *Dark turkey*
Thorax: *Same as body*
Legs: *Woodduck or substitute*

JANSSEN'S LEECH (Hal Janssen)

Hook: *Size 6 - 8, 2-4X Long*
Thread: *Black, olive, brown or gray*
Tail: *Marabou fibers to match thread, sparse*

Body: *Tying thread, thin*
Wings: *Marabou fibers, same as tail*
Head: *Marabou fibers dubbed onto thread*

JANSSEN'S THREAD FIN SHAD (Hal Janssen)

Hook: *Size 6, 3X long*
Thread: *Gray*
Tail: *Gray marabou fluff off of hackle*
Underbody: *Artboard or mattboard trimmed to shape*

Body: *Pearl mylar piping, painted gray on back*
Optics: *Eyes painted white with black pupils*

KAUFMANN'S TIMBERLINE EMERGER (Randall Kaufmann)

Hook: *Tiemco 5262 or 200, size 12 - 16*
Thread: *Olive or brown*
Tail: *Dark moose, sparse, or marabou, short and heavy*
Rib: *Copper wire*
Body: *Haretron, olive or brown to match thread*

Legs: *Brown neck hackle*
Wings: *Grizzly hen hackle tips*

Attention:
Wings should be tied short, approximately half the length of the body

◆◆◆◆◆◆◆◆

KAUFMANN'S STIMULATOR; October Caddis (Randall Kaufmann)

Body: *Rusty orange dubbing*
Wing: *Dark elk*
Thorax: *Yellow dubbing*
Hackle: *Grizzly*

Hook: *Size 6 - 8, 3X long*
Thread: *Fluorescent fire orange*
Tail: *Dark elk*
Rib: *Brown hackle*

KAUFMANN'S CHIRONOMID PUPA (Randall Kaufmann)

Hook: *Size 18 - 20*
Thread: *Black*
Tail: *Clear antron fiber, tied short*
Antennae: *same as tail*
Ribbing: *White silk thread*

Body: *Hairtron, black, slender*
Thorax: *Black hairtron*
Wing: *Wide grizzly hen hackle tip, tied one-third body length*

KAUFMANN'S CHIRONOMID LARVA (Randall Kaufmann)

Hook: *Size 18 - 20*
Thread: *Black*
Tail: *Antron fibers, sparse and short*
Antennae: *same as tail*

Body: *Hairtron, black, slender. Marabou is a good substitute*
Thorax: *Black hairtron*

Red Version
Hook: *Size 8 - 2*
Thread: *Fluorescent fire orange*
Body: *Fluorescent red chenille*
Hackle/Head: *Pearl Krystal Flash*

Attention:
1. Head is formed "bullet style" with remaining fibers trimmed to form hackle over the body

KRYSTAL BULLET (Robert Borden)

Green Version
Hook: *6 - 8*
Thread: *Fluorescent Green*
Body: *Chartreuse chenille*

Head and Hackle: *Black Krystal Flash tied bullet head style, length of shank*

LaFONTAINE'S EMERGENT SPARKLE PUPA (Gary LaFontaine)

**Brown and
Bright Green Version**
Hook: *12 - 14*
Thread: *Olive*
Overbody: *Olive sparkle yarn*

Underbody: *One-third olive sparkle yarn, two-thirds bright green craft fur*
Wing: *Brown Deer hair*
Head: *Brown marabou or dubbing*

◆━━◆━◆━◆━◆━◆

LEFTY'S DECEIVER White/Blue Version (Lefty Kreh)

Hook: *Mustad 3407, size 1/0 - 3/0*
Thread: *White, size A Nymo or equivilent*
Tail: *Six white saddle hackles, soft, one to one and a half times the length of the hook, tie in at end of shank. Add six strands of Flashabou to each side of the tail, same length*
Body: *Silver mylar wrapped nearly to the eye*

Collar: *Medium bunch of white bucktail, twice as long as hook, apply top and bottom of hook shank*
Topping: *Add small bunch of blue hair and peacock herl to cover the wing*
Head: *Tying thread*

Olive Version
Hook: *Mustad 3407, size 1/0 - 3/0*
Thread: *Green, size A Nymo or equivilent*
Tail: *Six to twelve white saddle hackles, soft, one olive dyed grizzly on each side. Add 10 to 12 strands of lime or gold Krystal Flash per side*
Body: *Silver mylar*

Beard: *Red Krystal Flash*
Collar: *White bucktail top and bottom of shank, one olive dyed grizzly hackle per side*
Topping: *Ten to 15 strands of peacock herl, 10 - 15 strands of lime green Krystal Flash*
Head: *Tying thread, painted yellow eye with black pupil is optional*

LEFTY'S DECEIVER (Lefty Kreh)

Yellow Version
Hook: *Mustad 3407, size 1/0 - 3/0*
Thread: *Yellow, size A Nymo or equivilent*
Tail: *Six to 12 yellow saddle hackles, add 10 to 12 strands of gold mylar per side*
Body: *Silver mylar*

Beard: *Red Krystal Flash*
Collar: *Yellow bucktail top and bottom of shank*
Topping: *Ten to 15 strands of peacock herl, 10 - 15 strands of gold Krystal Flash*
Head: *Tying thread*

LIGHT CAHILL (Dan Cahill)
Hook: *Size 16*
Thread: *Cream*
Wings: *Barred lemon wood duck*
Tail: *Light ginger hackle*
Body: *Cream Dubbing*
Hackle: *Light ginger*

LITTLE YELLOW STONE
Hook: *Size 14*
Thread: *Yellow*
Tail: *Light ginger, short*
Butt: *Rusty orange dubbing*
Body: *Yellow dubbing*
Wing: *White poly yarn, downwing style*
Hackle: *Light ginger, clipped top and bottom/trimmed on sides*

MARABOU DAMSEL
(Randall Kaufmann)
Hook: *Size 10*
Thread:2 Olive
Tail: *Olive marabou, pinch off short*
Ribbing: *Copper wire or olive thread*
Body: *Olive marabou tied in by tips, left over ends can form the wing*
Wingcase: *Olive marabou, extends one-third of body length*

MARTINEZ BLACK NYMPH (Don Martinez)

Hook: *Size 10 - 12, weight to suit*
Thread: *Black*
Tail: *Speckled guinea fibers*
Ribbing: *Oval copper tinsel*
Body: *Black angora goat*

Wingcase: *Green goose quill segment or raffia*
Thorax: *Black chenille*
Hackle: *Grizzly*

MATTHEW'S SPARKLE DUN (Craig Matthews)

Tan Version
Hook: *Size 16 - 18*
Thread: *Tan*
Wing: *Tan Deer body hair, tied upright and spread 180 degrees*

Tail: *Olive Z-Lon or Sparkle Poly*
Body: *Tan Dubbing*

Gray Version
Hook: *Size 16 - 18*
Thread: *Gray*
Wing: *Tan/gray Deer body hair, tied*
upright and spread 180 degrees
Tail: *Olive/brown Z-Lon or sparkle poly*
Body: *Gray dubbing*

Blue Winged Olive Version
Hook: *Size 16 - 18*
Thread: *Olive*
Wing: *Natural Deer body hair, tied*
upright and spread 180 degrees
Tail: *Olive-brown sparkle poly or Z-Lon*
Body: *Light - Medium olive dubbing*

Pale Morning Dun Version
Hook: *Size 16 - 18*
Thread: *Orange*
Wing: *Light dun deer body hair, tied*
upright and spread 180 degrees
Tail: *Olive/brown Z-Lon or sparkle poly*
Body: *Yellowish-orange dubbing*

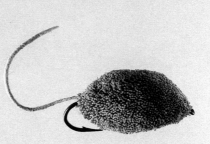

MOUSE

Hook: *Size 4, 3X long*
Thread: *Brown or gray*

Tail: *Chamois strip*
Body: *Deer hair, spun and clipped to shape*

◆━━◆━━◆━━◆

MUDDLER MINNOW (Dan Gaper)

Hook: *Size 6 - 10*
Thread: *Brown*
Tail: *Mottled brown turkey quill*
Body: *Flat gold tinsel*
Underwing: *Gray squirrel tail*

Wing: *Mottled turkey wing*
Hackle: *Spin on a collar of natural deer hair*
Head: *Spin on natural deer hair, clip to shape*

OLIVE MATUKA

Hook: *Size 6 - 10*
Thread: *Olive*
Ribbing: *Medium oval gold tinsel*
Body: *Olive chenille, dubbing, or yarn*

Wing: *Four dyed olive grizzly saddle hackles*
Collar (optional): *Grizzly died olive as a wet fly collar*

PALE MORNING DUN

Parachute Version
Hook: *Size 16 - 20*
Thread: *Cream*
Wing: *White poly yarn, loopwing*

Tail: *Light Dun or cream*
Body: *Light yellow*
Hackle: *Light Dun or cream, parachute*

PARACHUTE HARE'S EAR

Hook: *Size 14 - 16*
Thread: *Brown*
Wing: *White calf body hair*

Tail: *Natural deer hair*
Body: *Hare's mask dubbing*
Hackle: *Grizzly, parachute*

PHEASANT TAIL NYMPH (Al Troth)

Hook: *Size 12 -18, weight to suit*
Thread: *Brown*
Tail: *Ringneck pheasant, tail fibers*
Ribbing: *Copper wire*
Body: *Same as tail*

Wingcase: *Same as tail, left over wingcase tips are the legs, tied divided*
Thorax: *Peacock*

POLAR SHRIMP

Hook: *Size 6*
Thread: *Orange*
Tail: *Scarlet red hackle fibers*

Body: *Orange chenille*
Hackle: *Orange*
Wing: *White calf tail*

POLLY'S CASUAL DRESS (Polly Rosborough)

Hook: *Tiemco 300, size 8 - 14*
Thread: *Black*
Tail: *Bunch of muskrat fur, tie in short, leave guard hairs in*
Body: *Dubbed muskrat fur, noodle style, with guard hairs*

Collar: *Muskrat extending back one-third of body length*
Head: *Black ostrich, wide*

PRINCE NYMPH (Doug Prince)

Hook: *Size 10 - 14*
Thread: *Black*
Tail: *Brown goose biot*
Ribbing: *Oval gold tinsel*

Body: *Peacock*
Legs: *Brown partridge*
Wing: *White goose biot*

QUIGGLY CRIPPLE (Bob Quiggly)

Hook: *Size 16 - 20*
Thread: *Yellow 3/0*
Tail: *Olive to olive/brown marabou*
Rib: *Tying thread doubled*
Body: *Olive marabou or Ostrich herl*

Thorax: *Olive deer hair, spun*
Wing and Wingcase: *Dun deer hair or Elk hair*
Hackle: *Grizzly dyed olive*

ROYAL WULFF (Dan Bailey)

Hook: *Size 12 - 16*
Thread: *Black*
Wing: *White calf tail, or calf body hair*
Tail: *Elk hair, or moose body hair*

Body: *Peacock herl, divided by band of red floss*
Hackle: *Brown*

SCREAMIN' SHRIMP

Hook: *Mustad 3407, size 2 - 6*
Thread: *Fluorescent fire orange*
Tail: *White bucktail*
Antennae: *Remaining tips of tail plus pale orange Krystal Flash from carapace*
Tip: *Tying thread*
Eyes: *Medium bead chain, tied in above the barb*
Ribbing: *Gold wire*
Carapace: *Pale orange Krystal Flash*
Over Body: *Clear "V-Rib" or Larva Lace*
Body: *Fluorescent orange tying thread*

Attention:
1. Tie in white bucktail at eye of hook with tips extending past bend of hook
2. Wrap thread back down bend, wrap back up and tie in Krystal Flash for antennae. Wrap thread down bend then up to position over the barb
3. Tie in bead chain eyes over barb on the bottom of the hook shank
4. Tie in wire, carapace, and V-rib in that order
5. Taper the body with your tying thread, heavier at the rear and thin toward the eye
6. Wrap overbody of V-rib
7. Pull carapace over the top and rib with wire
8. Whip finish, trim bucktail and krystal flash about one quarter inch

69

SCUD (Fred Arbona)

Hook: *Size 10 - 14*
Thread: *Olive*
Tail: *Olive hackle fibers*
Shellback: *Clear 4mm plastic sheeting or Zip-Loc baggie strip*

Ribbing: *Clear monofilament 4X or 5X*
Body: *Olive dubbing, spun in a dubbing loop*

SCULPIN

Hook: *Size 4, 4X long*
Thread: *Olive*
Rib: *3X monofilament*
Body: *Olive yarn*
Wing: *Olive rabbit strip, ribbed with monofilament*

Pectoral Fins: *Olive deer hair*
Head: *Olive, brown and gray wool or deer hair, spun and clipped to shape*

Orange Version
Hook: *3908-C Mustad, size 2 - 8*
Thread: *Fluorescent fire orange*
Optics: *Medium silver bead chain*

Tail: *Fluorescent fire orange floss, 12 - 16 strands*
Body: *20 pound orange Amnesia*

SHAD FLY

Red Version
Hook: *3908-C Mustad, size 2 - 8*
Thread: *White or Red*
Optics: *Medium silver bead chain*

Tail: *White hackle fibers*
Body: *Silver mylar tinsel*
Collar: *Medium red chenille*
Hackle: *White*

71

SHAD FLY (Len Bearden)

Chartreuse Version
Hook: *3908-C Mustad, size 4 - 6*
Thread: *Fluorescent fire orange*
Optics: *Medium silver bead chain*
Tail: *Fluorescent green, 4 strand floss,*
     use 12 - 16 strands

Butt: *Tying thread*
Body: *Silver mylar tinsel*
Collar: *Tying thread*
Hackle: *Fluorescent yellow*

SILVER COMET

Hook: *Size 4 - 6*
Thread: *Yellow*
Tail: *Orange bucktail or calf tail*

Body: *Silver Diamond Braid*
Hackle: *Yellow and orange mixed*
Eyes: *Silver bead chain*

SILVER HILTON

Hook: *Size 6 - 10, weight to suit*
Thread: *Black*
Tail: *Barred mallard, tie in short*
Ribbing: *Oval silver tinsel*

Body: *Black chenille*
Wings: *Grizzly neck hackle tips, tie in "V" over the body*
Hackle: *Grizzly*

◆━━◆━━◆━━◆

SOFT HACKLE (Syl Nemes)

Lime Version
Hook: *Size 14 - 16*
Thread: *Green*
Body: *Green floss, or dubbing, thin*

Thorax: *Hare's ear dubbing*
Hackle: *Gray or brown partridge. Soft hen hackle may be substituted*

SOFT HACKLE (Syl Nemes)

Pheasant Tail Version
Hook: *Size 14 - 16*
Thread: *Black*

Body: *Pheasant tail*
Hackle: *Brown partridge*

◆━◆━◆━◆━◆

SPINNER, Rusty

Poly Winged Version
Hook: *Size 16 - 22*
Thread: *Brown*

Tail: *Cream or Dun hackle fibers, split and long*
Body: *Rust dubbing*
Wing: *White poly yarn*

SURF PERCHER (John Shewey)

Red Version
Hook: *Mustad 3407, size 2 - 6*
Thread: *Red*
Eyes: *Large bead chain*
Tail: *Yellow marabou, short*

Body: *Red Diamond Braid*
Wing: *Red marabou*
Over Wing: *Red krystal flash*
Beard (optional): *Yellow marabou*

THOR (Jim Pray)

Hook: *Size 6*
Thread: *Brown*
Tail: *Orange hackle fibers*

Body: *Red chenille*
Hackle: *Brown*
Wing: *White calf tail*

WHITE MARABOU MUDDLER (Dan Bailey)

Hook: *Size 2*
Thread: *Gray*
Tail: *Dyed red hackle fibers*
Body: *Flat silver tinsel, or silver Diamond Braid*
Wing: *White marabou, top with six strands of peacock herl*

Collar: *Spun natural deer hair*
Head: *Spun and trimmed natural gray deer hair*

Attention: Weight to suit for use in saltwater

WHITLOCK BLACK ANN (Dave Whitlock)

Hook: *37187 Mustad, Stinger, size 6*
Weedguard: *Hard monofilament, same diameter as hook*
Tail: *4 Black hackle feathers, half length of hackles, blue and black rubber hackle*

Hackles: *Black*
Body: *Black deer hair, blue deer hair middle band, white deer hair face, spun and clipped*
Legs: *Black rubber hackle*
Optics: *6mm doll eyes, tinted blue*

WHITLOCK EELWORM STREAMER (Dave Whitlock)

Purple Version
Hook: *Tiemco 7999 or Mustad 36890, size 4 - 6*
Weedguard: *Hard nylon, same diameter as hook*
Optics: *Medium/large silver bead chain*

Tail: *2 to 4 slender saddle hackles, grizzly dyed purple,3 times the length of hook*
Body: *Coarse dubbing, dyed purple*
Rib: *Wide soft hackle, grizzly dyed purple, tied palmered*
Head: *Coarse dubbing, same as body*

WHITLOCK CRAYFISH (Dave Whitlock)

Hook: *Tiemco 300, size 4 - 10, weighted*
Thread: *Color to match body*
Optics: *Burned monofilament or black nylon beads*
Antennae: *Two strands of dark moose*
Nose (tail): *Dyed deer hair to match body*
Pinchers: *Speckled hen hackle feathers on top, cream hen underneath, glued together*

Rib: *Copper wire*
Legs: *Grizzly hackle dyed to match body*
Body: *Antron blend, color to suit (orange, brown, etc), sides picked*
Tail and Back: *Raffia to match body*
Highlights: *Use Pantone pen to finish any detailing*

WOOLLY WORM, Black

Hook: *Size 6*
Thread: *Black*
Tail: *Red yarn, short*

Hackle: *Grizzly saddle tied palmered over the body*
Body: *Black chenille*

WOOLLY BUGGER, Black

Hook: *Size 6*
Thread: *Black*
Tail: *Black marabou blood feathers*
Ribbing: *Black saddle hackle, palmered through body*

Body: *Black chenille*

Attention: Weight to suit

YELLOW HUMPY (Jack Horner)

Hook: *Size 12 - 14*
Thread: *Yellow*
Tail: *Moose body hair*
Underbody: *Yellow thread*

Body: *Natural deer hair*
Wing: *Formed from pulled over deer hair*
Hackle: *Brown and grizzly mixed*

YELLOW JACKET

Hook: *Size 10 - 12*
Thread: *Brown*
Body: *Dirty yellow dubbing*

Rib: *Black thread*
Wings: *Brown hackle tips*
Hackle: *Brown*

ZONKER (Al Troth, style)

Natural Version
Hook: *Mustad 9674, size 6 - 8*
Thread: *Black and Red*
Underbody: *Metallic tape, trimmed to minnow shape*
Body: *Silver mylar tubing*

Butt or Tag: *Red thread used to tie in mylar near bend, and to secure wing to body*
Wing: *Strip of natural brown/gray rabbit fur*
Hackle: *Grizzly*
Head: *Black*

◄━━◆◆◆━━►

ZUG BUG (Cliff Zug)

Hook: *Size 8 - 14*
Thread: *Black*
Tail: *Peacock sword, short*
Ribbing: *Oval silver tinsel*

Body: *Peacock herl*
Hackle: *Brown or partridge, as a beard*
Wingcase: *Barred lemon wood duck*